LADDER MUSIC

T0161986

Also by Ellen Doré Watson

Broken Railings
(Green Lake Chapbook Prize)

We Live in Bodies

The Alphabet in the Park:
Selected Poems of Adélia Prado
(translations)

LADDER
MUSIC

POEMS BY

Ellen Doré Watson

ALICE JAMES BOOKS
Farmington, Maine

Acknowledgments

The author gratefully acknowledges the editors of the journals in which these poems first appeared (sometimes in earlier renditions):

Agni: "More Than Anything I Like to Sing But It's Rare"
American Poetry Review: "The Year to Come"
Marlboro Review: "Too Many Ladybugs Smelling of Turmeric"
Poetry Northwest: "Hypothermia"
Prairie Schooner: "Another Landscape" (as "Life Goes On")
Sanctuary: The Journal of the Massachusetts Audubon Society: "River Road"

Many thanks to those who have been instrumental in the revising and re-imagining of these poems, especially Agha Shahid Ali, Annie Boutelle, Amy Dryansky, Mary Koncel, Carol Potter, Margaret Szumowski, April Ossmann, Suzanne Wise, and Barbara Ras.

Thanks also to the Rona Jaffe Foundation and to the Massachusetts Cultural Council for time and space to make this book.

Alice James Books gratefully acknowledges support from the University of Maine at Farmington and the National Endowment of the Arts.

10 9 8 7 6 5 4 3 2 1

Alice James Books are published by the Alice James Poetry Cooperative, Inc., an affiliate of the University of Maine at Farmington.

ALICE JAMES BOOKS
238 Main Street
Farmington, ME 04938
ww.umf.maine.edu/~ajb

Library of Congress Cataloging-in-Publication Data
Watson, Ellen, 1950-
    Ladder music: poems / by Ellen Doré Watson.—1st ed.
    p. cm.
    ISBN 1-882295-30-7 (pbk.)
    I. Title.

PS3573.A8523 L33 2001
811'.54--dc21   2001046185

For my mother—
Marion Doré Watson

Contents

ONE

Imperfect Knowledge

I know wind and water are at their worst
together, horizontal, I know air
so dry mirrors refuse to fog, skin
falls in scales. Even sleeping I know
paper from cloth, windows from ledges,
I can and do read maps. I know the soil
I grew in and the frequency of watering
but which leaves shall I shed? I've known bulk
and I've known threadbare, but how to know
if three chairs at my table is enough?
I know the crow, I know the branches,
I do not know the culvert.
I know the cellar, wet and mousy,
I know the attic nails reaching for my head,
cotton candy coming out the seams.
But has my glass ever been utterly empty
or full? I know to drain it, but not
who to ask about the long tunnel of light.

No One Else

So much of the world moans or glitters and I refuse
to close my eyes. Is this living or being distracted?
Consider that it's March, a hard month not to think
about time. Who would want to be mud season,

barely hope, nothing much to look at? Of course, open
or closed, my eyes are weakening like everything else.
Aging, we sink underwater, time pressure per square inch
exploding exponentially. Forget sponges and featherdusters,

everything should lick itself clean. Forget feeding the fire,
paying the bills. Mixed greens should come washed and crisp
and stay that way. No time to saw at each other, no shopping,
cover the mirrors. Time to get serious about what matters,

chief among which is the search for ways to slow the plummet
to the ocean floor. Sewing parachutes, building arm muscles
that ripple, finding a safe pouch for fear, these things take time.
The thing about finding your balance is no one else can do it.

Freight

I followed a truck of guns to work today,
crates lashed to a flatbed, dash of red
FRAGILE and taillights. Ugly March buffered
and air-brushed by fog, sun making promises
from offstage, but walking around my head:
the ones that particular freight would kill how long
from now. Shadow futures—people in the middle
of their morning lives, shaking flakes into a bowl,
punching out to go home—suddenly voiced
in the diamond click and roar of studded snows
beneath me, in the flash of Paul beneath me—
my breasts in his hands immortal or at least
our love. In Della, calming beneath my wide
mother hand, unloading the day's cruelties, kids
with their own invisible bullet holes who shoot hurt
like buckshot. Sometimes she knows her stories pale
beside the size of, say, *The Winter of Red Snow.*
Some days she has to shut the book, stop
the seeping sadness, no matter whose. Today I flare
and think to run this truck off the road, wish it a colorful
crash and burn, stacks of virgin rifles steaming, ruined,
all those expectant trigger fingers forced to make a fist and
do their damage with flesh. Wonder and cringe when this
thought brings me flaming fingertips, hands that are mine
bursting to do hurt. And my ready right foot, my two-bit
dream of making kids and deer and dairy marts safe
for a sweet month! I watch my hands turn the wheel, the car
veers off onto the highway's shoulder, all the anger
of a Monday morning mysteriously leavened
by a few spirals of fog and a little sense—me
working to hold the driver blameless, the truck, this day,
it's a job, it could just as well be cabbages he's hauling.

Green Whistles

Green whistles at me while you
my love are off nudging a car
across the map of Pennsylvania.
Eyes on the road! Fear I suppose
must be peeked at but mostly I lock it
in the dark. From my own sudden
quiet static blooms. I'm thinking
of the jangle winter air makes my body
(now a green sound) do. Nothing like
these small leaves' *shimmy shimmy*
on their slim stems. Trouble exists, even

when you don't go there—like the reproach
of bark, darker than leaves, sturdy
and resentful. What if my 'I love you'
isn't big enough to bring you back?
Is worry why I'm wearing flowers?
Fear is a stubborn stain, ornery river.
Of course trucks are headed this and
every way, but gauging speed and impact
won't keep them out of my lane, your lane.
In good soil up to my wrists, I think
maybe instead of lighting up I should

touch myself every time I need a smoke.
I look up. The world is finally more
green than yellow. Our nine-year-old
is more mine this week than ever.
Ever since I resolved to live *andante*
inside each measure of this fast song
I've learned that looking makes
a melody of rote; knowing your feet
is like belief. Della has her copper beech
and her body—and knows both have many
rooms. Geese sliding on silent mirrors

have bullfrog accompaniment, fray of songbirds,
much work to do with their eager young,
and all this they know more keenly than fear.
I can't help myself. I'm sorry for the roots
as I press down the stake, sorry for the dark
kingdoms I bludgeon with light.
Sorry for the way this morning I thought
"Paul" and "eighteen-wheeler" in the same
sentence, and since I don't know how to pray
to upstairs, I pray you instead. Let superstition
apply only to luck. Let me be what I was

at the opera—joyous and perverse, ears a-dream,
eyes keen on the conductor's heels floating up and up
off the floor as elbows and vocal chords heaved
and sawed before him, and the *thwipp! thwipp!*
as flat green blades suggesting plants disappeared
down their slots in the stage. So much is music.
If I let them, the shrubs have ears, soft ones,
cocked and waiting for sunset. Living in Della's eyes
I learn new ways not to lie. Living in your absence
is like becoming you—I rout field grass with pitchfork,
loving the word itself, then doze on the couch, remote

in my hand. (Though I'll need you home soon
to explain people who paint stones). Right now,
in full slantwise sun, fear's a pea in my pocket—
though I can't help but notice the shadow
now dwarfs the tree, and it's too chill a day
for it to translate as inviting, and there aren't enough
flashbulbs or good thoughts in the world to make it
go away. You'll be okay. When the birds screech
and divebomb, instead of *portent* I think: imagine
the first time dissonance was more than a wrong
note! Nothing needs a paint job in this light.

Mind's Teacup

Time in the wind's chariot, invisible
then gone. Fear in the blind

surrey, a wagonload, an endless
road. Ashes in the wind's

vanishing, we bless
the fingers' residue. Eggs

in the moment's wagon—mystery,
hope, and danger triple-belted,

making friends. Worry in the star's
chamber: in the astral wheelbarrow,

is there enough room? Work is not
enough, nor eggs nor tippy. Blue

of the body's muffler, the way
that word cuts both ways. Ash

in the mind's teacup, no one
sipping. Tomorrow in the body's

garden, possibility of curdling.
Learning in the skin's vessel,

music doing the making. Once
in a blue day, enough in now's

fragile room.

Universally

I am not a prayer plant, I am in no way
a teapot. It's all just
hot water, said my mouth sheepishly,
turning back a lifetime of proffered
trays: lovely little cups of dark
grounds, fired clay someone's hands loved
long enough to make into money,
tiny screen molded to hold
something once green, steep it
into comfort—

(Why *should* the wind agree to be soothing?
The trees are a bundle
of protestations, universally.
I am not your mother, groans
the earth, shaking blocks of apartments
down on people. What do we *take*
her for?)

—a flock of wool shrugs on the hill waiting
to be gathered.
A patch of cement gives way
to tolerant crabgrass.
Under the lawn the gnawed
bulbs keep on preparing yellow.

The Year to Come

Prairie dog, totem pole, cluster
of grapes: do we choose our omens
or they us? I think I see tunnels, painted
faces turning wooden, dew on each perfect
globe. (Industry, artifice, sexlovefood?)
I see the way we're speeding up and they're
breaking down. This year on its way to us
on greased rails your father will die

and my mother will worsen. A year
faces forward like a paper doll but all
the color's on the back side. Which is worse:
that he will die again next year and the year after
or that she will not, sliding and sliding?
I see a piano in yawning stillness, then a daughter
whose music fills the house. A glassed aviary
circled by wheel chairs. I will light small fires

to thaw the slippery slope. Steep I can handle
and dirty. Our bodies will become mirrors,
heaving to the same hurt. This we can like,
and how our centerpiece gives off light,
our good fruit. I keep seeing that kitten
mothered by Roxie the Great Dane. I keep
smelling that hallway, room after room
of TV noise and withered hands dabbing at eyes

no one wants to look into really. A year
is like a fortune cookie and do you have to eat it
every bit, for it to come true? Spun sugar
folded around the outcome but where
has Confucius gone—nowadays only flattery

and *your lucky numbers* in a red string.
Just like a new girlfriend, you keep thinking
you've got to pretend each year is prettier

than all the ones before. I'm on the look-out
for the perfect early warning system, a wooden
remembrance, anything purple. This year niece
number three will tiptoe—we *will* this to be so—
towards survival, relearning to take, eat, this food
is broken for you, for you not to be broken, even if
someone has bound more than your feet. There is
so much we don't know. I'm thinking

we should wear our welcoming faces
so the year can slip into us whatever way
it wants to. Like the night somebody else's
two-year-old found the way from his private
dark to our unfamiliar bodies in his parents'
bed, blinked at us, puzzled, and proceeded
to close his eyes, burrow a place between us—
his warm, unexpected weight—that kind of gift.

Doubting Instinct

I'm doubting instinct, this bullfrog frozen
silent in blasting heat, big mud lump assuming
the safety of camouflage, danger of me—

a hugeness turned toward its rustle and thud.
Without a rhythmic baseline, my ears tune
to background: distant hammering and high up,

a jet tearing bandages from the bright bed linen
of the sky. From across sun-stunned lawns comes
the noise of children, very plural, a class of them

like bubbles frothing over and around each shiny
other, snuffable and sure as fire leaping, together
a brush fire, one rising call like a single moment's

highest licking flame. Yesterday this elementary
noise would have faded from intrusion to wrap-around,
present or invisible as pounding surf; today their far

voices don't sound different but mean
different, now we know a thirteen-year-old
can inhabit rage so eloquent, rage so unintelligible

as to kill many and fast and not know why. Why
does this frog refuse to move, seem to want me
to meddle? I wish her away from the bank's pounded

brown, back to familiar muck and song. I watch
the geese skate the pond, playing Simon Says
with five fuzzballs they think they can keep safe.

TWO

Attempted Prayer

Help me, Spirit of the Possible, I'm no good
at this. Body at rest and the rest of me lost
forty years back in the grain of the oak pew
behind my bare legs, in the hum of many mouths,
memory grinding out a formula for solace.
O Possible Spirit, I'm self-confessed, well-wrapped
in the inconsistent music of my days—it's later
and elsewhere I worry. Like the trip-wire life
can pull taut between brothers, and how will they
cross the street? Like the many feet slapping down
the path to the water hole—no land mines today, please.
There goes my pager and I'm half an hour too far
from frail Edwina and her husband holding his hat.
They need You now. And in Haiti fuzz-cheeked G.I.s
eye edgy crowds, cradle their guns, mull over
instructions to use their judgment. Give them some.

All or Nothing

One hand opens only if the other closes.
It's the symmetry of nature: blossom, riverbed,
lightning. We think about this straight-ahead—
if we do at all: she parts with the Blue Willow
because of Chinese tin, not filling with new song.
If B. can't come to dinner, eat Y. What about
the word *all*, the word *nothing*? Together,
they make a toast in Brazil. In the face
of too much, the gut says *get little*. Revert
to bare floors, move to Rangoon, swim
in three days' silence, nothing but soup.
What would happen if I refused to look
at my feet? Stayed in one place, spinning?
Hands un-full, un-empty: new butterflies. . .

Fruit

"Slightly is not fatal, a hornet does not a fever make."

Once was a girl born wanting
to eat beauty. Who was taught
improvement is the collision
between clearly and enough.
And lo, the sun shone and she
was fed, loved. Cleansing ever
the assignment, much suds,
the word rugged. When it comes
to bodily, even flawless peaches
are either forever before or beyond
perfection—so, hup-to, ten-hut!
That's why we believe in God
and nectarines! And so the girl
marched, anti-marched, moved out,
resolutely bought peaches and ate them
naked. Gave herself to other small
betrayals that seemed like bending
for good reason to bad light.
She read books, fascinated by nuts
and stingers, shades and severals,
unmasked untils and alls—bodily
abstractions that handed over fever,
pure wasp, pure pulp. Teachers that said
choice, said she might attract danger, yield
to a hand, juice a beautiful mouth. At last,
a fate she can live with: fruit—fleet perfection
discovered on the windowsill in a small brown
bag. More than slightly worth it, then gone.

September in Three Parts

1

Gone are the green parrots, impossible
in Bridgeport filling limbs already full
with apples beside the ferry boat. Gone
are the days she would fall asleep on my chest,
or almost. Gone the groundhog and much
of our broccoli. Some things slip away,
some go out all showy, others need to be
pushed heaving and sweating. Gone
is the dodo bird, the sticker we didn't put
on her lunch box because "dodo" and "Della"
are too close for comfort in a school
with Sally Backstrom. Gone is my mother's
dream of seeing the Taj Mahal, though
she could grab it back, couldn't she,
like her eyesight? Gone is her authority,
invisibly; Dad's giving his away. Wills
and last wishes like acorns for someone
else's winter: gone the green.

2

This morning on the radio a white buffalo was born
and Lakota Sioux flocked in great plumes
of September dust because the creature
on the white man's ranch was no albino mutant
but had brown eyes: the sacred sign
that we have 20 years to clean up our mess.
"What's new?" we ask at parties or
straddling the crack on the sidewalk,
instead of *what matters*? What's new is
faster smaller lighter brighter. *To wish*
for a killing frost—simply to call a halt
to sneezing—that's a new one on me.

3

The strains of music in her head stayed.
They'd pulse and glide at odd moments,
she'd call the melody sometimes
and it would come, neatly brushed dog
to lick her face. Pain can have that kind of echo.
Well-aimed words that wound, semi-automatic.
Motherness lasts long after a child has been wrenched
away—there are women with eyes to prove it.
Water goes on rolling, invisible waves of vapor
the clouds eat up and throw down. The trees are our lungs,
wood turns to stone, it's all a kind of saving grace
even when we've lost our keys, our footing, our place
in line. It's part of the plan that we don't know
who'll outlast who. The worms aerate the waiting
soil, fire lives in flint. Can we look around
at this frayed beauty and say hope or fury die?
Love and last night's supper stop breathing,
change places, and go on.

Before Bed

The word I leave out on the stoop to shiver
like a cat that tears up a couch in the night
is *forget*. I don't want it in my dreams.
The dreams can be themselves terrifying or
gone in the morning, just as long as they remember
everything as long as they last. I don't stoop down
before bed as I was taught by my forgetting mother
who is learning to be gone, trying to remember
to dream as long as she lasts, like the cat on a cold stoop
dreams of a good, stuffed couch, morning's open door.
I shiver in my tears, *forget* in my hand, say *shoo*.

Certain of the Water

I've forgotten how to be a root, a mole
in the earth reaching toward dark. How to
labor, mute, without sun on my face.
Do roots have shadows? Can music cast light?
I'm sitting in the shadow of a large someone,
a verb tense with my name on it, what an overhang.
I am a guest in my own thoughts, it's not like me
to wear a hat. A good guest needs solitude, leaves
her host time to chop wood and garlic, a good
excuse. I join the throng gasping and eating popcorn,
we like it when the spangles and muscled bodies slip
from the silver necklace and bounce
in the net. Other people's risks are what
bring us under the big top, we leave our shadows
outside. Whose are the hands I should trust
to catch my wrists, tunnel my dark, tender
my bread? Back home, I need a floor-plan,
a plumber, with a drought like this.
First wood and sun marry, that's the good part.
Then ruts are worn to washboard, capillaries strain
deeper like roundworms in the gut of the ground.
There's just no stew stewing. Some kind of blockish
cheer has gone on too long, certain of the water
in the pipes. I sit at the window, trying to invent
a string to pull, to loosen the sky.

She Forgets Aphasia

She forgets aphasia and all of Asia
She remembers Bangkok and birch bark, babies
She forgets the cats' names, clocks gone cock-eyed
She remembers doubt and doing something useful
She forgets even the Doxology
She remembers forgetting and several Franks
She forgets getting out of bed for a reason
She remembers having said grace but not how
She forgets "I"
She remembers Jim, jetty and Jesus
She forgets knitting but not his kindness
She remembers learning is lost, but oh can she laugh
She forgets me, maybe I'm a relation
She remembers not needing him—or maybe not
She forgets opinions, says oh
She remembers peaches, calling me one
She forgets questions used to have answers
She remembers remembering, rather vaguely
She forgets sunlight, stays safe inside
She forgets towels, how to fold them
She remembers under, used to go there
She forgets vanity
She remembers the Women's Christian Temperance Union
She forgets X the instant it's over
She forgets to wonder Y
She forgets to zip her pants but not to unzip her face:
A zinnia

Hummingbirds are Never Confused

A darting whir towards thin sweetness—look!
We welcome them into any arena: the blinding
still life out there where we'd like to go or
a dismal back yard full of junked bikes
or a full-tilt patio argument—all
become lightened, brightened, confused
by such goodness, apparent and fragile.
A rat looks out from under the tumble-down
house next door, eyes like rivets, thinks:
color overload in miniature, dithering.
Doesn't venture out. Okay I made him up.
What an idea, what a place to put
the other, the self. But invariably
while a bird like that hums, gyrating
its unfeathers, we find a way to glory,
then pout. Why can't we buy one?
(Why don't we know who we are?)

Cheese

Cheese for breakfast—at home never a thought of it
before noon, but Lorraine has started something;
Thursdays at ten, walking under her wisteria, hunger
is specific. Meant for some creature's babe, the milk
that would be this cheese was spritzed into metal,
plumped, rested, and dilled into a state of mouth-watering
and it's what I need. I'm a dry sponge in the hangover
wind and part of this day will be about finding water
everywhere I go: in the fake air of big stores, in the finger-
wagging office, the tin box of the car, in the high
temple of bodily where I and a dozen strangers
will use electricity to make nothing but holy
sweat. But first, let the cattails into the picture,
the trees' green bangles, the pond with no fixed color
but shine. The earth spongy with ant kingdoms,
the scat so dry and precise, the plain brown bird.
This is the world cheese is made of. Say grace.

THREE

Art & Ornament

Rocks nailed to sheet rock, bones
driven through skin, gardenia perched
on curve of ear. The way even
adolescents' boredom gives way
to loveliness. Every creature
in the house vies for the spot
of sun just now examining
the rug. Ornament, ego,
leisure: we kill and die for less
than this. The soloist goes out front
waiting to be swallowed.

Weathering Music

How unnerved we get doing something
new with eyes around threatening to narrow—
something we undergo like the knife, a reluctant

choice. Taking a dance class, first time driving
a snowy road, scarves of white smoke curling the tar,
brush-edged like a ginger cat, fur changing from root

to tip: milk white, ash gray, saffron yellow. Like
who we are, shifting weight and fashion, layers
thrown off, pulled on at the whim of clouds and sun,

identities altered by hair cuts, bad air, bitter words,
new berries. Sudden just desserts, old crevices,
strategies of honeysuckle or Achilles' heel. How we

orchestrate the I, take the sour notes to bed, clutched
to an idea of skid fin or seaworthy, weaving new themes
and wild hairs to a music that will weather well.

O

O sudden and occasional blue
O cello
O moments devoted solely to texture
Thank you for the wordless times
when instead of my brain it's my body
that won't let me out of my body
O moonlight
O dumb and beautiful chicken
I promise to eat you
To my feet some day in a hot place
I promise cool brown tiles
and to my shadow self standing there
air that stirs all of a person
bringing, the way it licks us, our skin
closer to others', so that sex walks around
glad-handing and available, not the once-
in-awhile toboggan of New England
O New England, where a whole town can slide
down the farmer's hill on its can of a Saturday night
O reason for embers, remember bicycles
and how viney we'll be by mid-June and
before that cold frames and sweet sap
O rusty earthmover
O perfect, imported grape

River Road

Because I'm tight-shouldered, speeding down
River Road, I take a breath of morning and think
what to praise. Such an old-fashioned,
churchly word, says a brain-path I choose
not to take because my eyes are full of river.
Praise rivers! The generosity of rivers, the way
they offer themselves up, as this one just did, and
the ways we can ride them—wet or blind, lolling
or studied—to a hearth or a campfire or a thought.
Praise their sturdy banks for standing, feeling time
pass through our bodies, praise roads that follow
their curves, the glint and sweetness of accompanying
them when we can. Praise the sleepy brain circuitry
that chose this alternate route: I could be chugging by
a campus that insists on chapel in blue blazers,
I could be looking at signs for Yamaha and taffy,
instead of markers for five varieties of seed corn.
Praise the gone crops to the left and to the right
and the cemetery in a box surrounded by stubble.
Fields fenced, unfenced, or bouldered, silt with its
history of water; porches and clapboard, racy
leaves losing chlorophyll. Praise rust for beauty:
baler, plow, and harrow. Praise every single
silo and brave fall rose. Praise this river tomorrow
for rain, now for this changeling morning,
loose and full-throated and tardy.

More Than Anything I Like to Sing But It's Rare

If nothing else, I know how to make a good fuss.
But I didn't want centrifugal force, I wanted
a flowering tree. Of my entire family, I'm the one
who loves red and leaves doors open.
The truth is I stand in awe of the human machine.
I peer into people's bodies in the back of the ambulance.
I sit with my breath and my recipes. I can't speak
for the monochromatic. Excuse the expression,
but there is such a thing as owning, it's just not
about money. I don't know about the arabesques
my limbs have never described. I didn't say flute,
I said cello. Short of wearing a club, joining a uniform,
what do I do with my big noise, to make it
surely music? I am sad without leaves.
And meanwhile, the world turns breezily in its rusty socket.
The trouble with green is it starts yellow
and ends brown. The trouble with green is
it's so dangerously quiet.

Chant

I'm forty-five and it was a foolish hope, but I accepted
    another month's blood, another cosmic *no*,
with at least a little bit of grace; then just hours later
    a startling red flower, this one from my throat,
new proof I am dying more than being born. How can it be,
    this bloom on white tissue, how can fire live
in wet hay, how can I put this blaze to good use, burn
    the yellow tallow of my body, parts I'd have done with,
and rise like ash? How can I refuse these flickering thoughts
    and stop shielding my eyes? I want to live inside
the voices at the Buddhist wedding, inside the lotus flower,
    I want to burrow into yesterday's wonder at the raw solace
of ritual music from human throats and my frail friend's new love,
    blessed by pyramids of grapefruit and nine sips of sake,
and that chattering sound swelling and wrapping me in the trees
    with the howler monkeys who don't know why.

But there's a sputtering flame in my chest and the whole world
    looks combustible, because of three days consumed
by phone calls and blood where it doesn't belong, because
    a woman in Vermont waking and sleeping sees a spray
of buckshot catch her son's shirt on a raft in Peru, his body
    tumbling into frothy rapids going red. Because red,
because a man named John, because he went and skied expertly
    into a tree, because Nancy is left stammering to her son
that Daddy's fire went out before they got him down the mountain
    the ski patrol scribbling DRT, Dead Right There, because
too much red, the fire of our lives leaking away, because fire
    eats and eats and has the bad manners to smack its lips,
gluttonous, indiscriminate. Fear is not a fire but burns in the back
    of my throat. I will not listen to my body today. Except
for the serene cells still dancing up and down like jaw after jaw
    in the temple making that throaty music from wild faith.

Natural

The leaves are coming down in huge bunches now
   (all I can think is hair after chemo), and we're to believe
     the death around the corner of December is natural—
because it happens unstoppably, because it unhappens
   when earth tires of being stone, when liquid comes alive
     in the heartwood, the topsoil, so we've got to swallow
our medicine now, break out the scrapers and mittens
   and salute the natural order, which will mean at least
     one ice storm per county, racking up 4.5 highway deaths
whether or not highways are natural, or the jaws of life,
   for that matter, which is what's got its teeth around my
     mother's wrist, holding on, her soul meanwhile
stalled out on the dark road right there in her living room
   where her feet dig in, her knees unlock, she must be
     dragged to her chair, she must be as tired of this
as her dragger, who is informed at monthly appointments
   that this is a natural progression, even the newest
     wrinkle: his sweetheart's wordless refusal
of the muffin he offers up to her clenched mouth,
   just as for years he offered his parishioners grape juice,
     little squares of white bread, the promise of eternal life.

Another Landscape

Following the Mississippi up the border of Wisconsin we see
in a couple hours maybe fifty-five deer slung into trucks,

swinging from trees, men in orange setting off into the woods
or cradling their darling guns. You think I have an attitude?

I'm fascinated by these men from the age of wool who eat meat
hacked and dressed out behind the A & W where my daughter

sipping root beer and staring at her first dead deer is without irony
handed a copy of *Bambi*. Coastal folk, what do we know

about the ambush of winter under a big sky? The hills' shoulders
—which, shrugging or heaving, made this place—give up the ghost

and leave us in rolling flatlands again. We've come to see afflicted
people we love and to say thanks to the place our food is grown

and killed, domestic. After the feast, the farm at night is wrapped
in a thin blowing snow, another landscape I can't completely enter,

reject, or romanticize. The pitch of the barn gives out hog snorts.
A distant plow scrapes at beauty so tomorrow the world can work.

The Sounds Between What's On My Mind

The woodstove sucks the wet out of us
so we need one more electric thing humming.
Where will my thoughts go, without night noises
to lead them—without the gnaw and racket
of Della's guinea pigs, sounding a lot like

mother love (and will she one day find mine
incessant?), without the bubbler to remind me
this man who loves his single goldfish deserves
always more than I have. Without my ears
I know streamers and balloons are softly

sagging in the living room, birthday whisperings
about decline, as I know two brothers
caught in a circle on a wood floor,
not wrestling. Even with this blasted machine,
there's a howling in the chimney and paws

on the roof; danger is no more or less real.
I was awake to see my baby, fat and happy,
when they cut her out of me, but still
they took something I'll never get back—
my best chance to learn the bodily

meaning of *yield*. Wind is the sound
of the world refusing to budge. In Casper,
Wyoming, there's always a 25 MPH gale and more
people kill themselves than anywhere else.
Before sleep, the things I would change

line up under my forehead. Blazing in the dark,
my resolve seems so loud, but I haven't learned
how to coax it to daylight, where it's sullen
and only smolders. The way smoke above the house
lofts upward, then floats down like a dirty cloak.

Five Words of Human Music

ANTHEM

Song as proof, song as threat—collective
warmth in the feel-good belly—anthems
can be dangerous music: chain-link

with other-drum singers rounded up behind.

PROOF

How complete unto itself, the music
of geometry. If this, then that, here
are the blues, there's the pudding.

I am proof of nothing alone. You are
proven, he is not. Human proving takes
time, not faith. Which do you have more of?

Where's the math in music?

BRAID

To braid is human.
Hair, a gleaming loaf, the taming of.
A way of thought, head music.

The rhythm of one long plait, plot
down a length of back, or braids
squat and bouncing, second-graders

down the hall. Fingers crossed, knotted
chains, a meditation of fingers producing
curls: separateness made evidence.

SOLO

Is the goal to solo, solving the proof of the "I"
or is it more heavenly to make perfection
in concert, three-men-in-a-boat?

Choosing a path, some see beauty in circles,
others follow exclamation points, dot-to-dot.

Listen, are we alone in our quandry—
or can animals be said to sing?

CHORD

Ah—simultaneous prongs, blessed wordless.
A rising above, strummed or plunked or
fingered: made of separate-but-equal.

The plural sound—a trinity—
that can close the book or leave it gaping open,
proof we love hairy joy and disquiet both.

Word Door

For Scottie Parsons,
  after her painting of the same name

Transom light, boxed, bright,
presiding spirit that rains down
the indigo dust our feet kick up
in this thought neighborhood.
Each of our days should have
one scarlet sentinel breaking
the rule of horizontal, a flaming
breadstick to stand beside, feeling
bullish and almost ready to brave
the door to the back room, door
to the deep. Always it's a skinny
space to shimmy into sideways,
but solid magnetic. And all around,
the storefront of evidence, promise
of color, the way sullied white
is a nakedness leaking through
and loudly, the feathery blue
stew of window remembering wet
and changeable. Delicate graffiti
that points to where we hope to find
ourselves, scritching on brilliance.

FOUR

Naming It

Am I silly, i.e. full of helpless help in a world
of troubles, to want to know the name
of the baby boy in Chicago whose muscles
they say will fail him, the name
of every mother's son, father's sunflower
in need of Miracle-Gro, stop-time,
redo? We've all met true need, after all,
in the neighborhood: the lanky, tall
family folded into a small dark house,
as if brick were protection, sun danger.
I'm not one of those who—bless them—
make casseroles and earnest petitions
to a personal savior—if anything hovers,
it strikes me as plural and cloud-like—
so what use would I make of a name
for any of this or the baby? We've learned
to make of a place a new adjective
—*Kossavar*—but until we're "it"
blood is no relative. My own troubles,
peas dried and treated into seeds,
don't—goodness knows—give me
enough to go on, so lucky,
so far. Outsize sorrow is like Welsh:
too many consonants, no matter who
they belong to. Someplace in my chest
where my own tiny mortality resides
is our collective longing—for a name to say
loud and often, the power of a vowel.

Rung

A dowel, round as sound and darkened
by my thoughts.
One after another seeming
likeness, unlikely vehicle.
Rungs of desire, where it gets you.
What a bell has done,
might do again, as in song.
What she did with her hands
while her face closed.
The hurt that seeing sang in my chest.
Wood.

Too Many Ladybugs Smelling of Tumeric

Colors true, chill air quick-sunned
back to balmy—this would be a good day
to be happy. I choose to settle
on what's in reach (out of synch

and momentary as this weather).
I'm half-way between a spring chicken
and a geezer, and suddenly alone
in the bright feedlot. This would be

a good day for speeding tickets, too,
but I'm of no mind to go anywhere.
I make an omelet and eat it outside
where so much is so inappropriately

alive, a big peek at yesterday's and
tomorrow's hidden. Ladybugs catch
in my hair. They know better than we
how long they have, their bug-brains done

with eating and fucking (it's call di-
apause); they leave yellow juice on my lap
(which my neighbor tells me is blood
bled from their joints), and that bad-dirt

smell—nothing but predators and shelter
left in their synapses: a frenzy of whirring
and jostling as they mount mass assaults
on the house's every orifice, hundreds of them

flattened in the door jambs as if fleeing
a nightclub fire. Poor tiny tortoises, late
October freckles on the screen, dark memory
of locusts, too much in a time of not-enough.

Magic

There is the memory of the child at two, saying
I know what magic is: magic is when you think
you can't do it and then you *do* do it.
There is the woman to whom this could never
happen. There is the woman stung in mid-summer,
awake with the birds, smoking, and the woman listening
to Callas who has left her behind. There is the mother
eating her tears, basting her child, biting her tongue,
and the memory of the child at four, saying God
made Moms and Dads and then gave them
his magic, and their magic is to make kids.
There are the arms of the child, older now,
encircling the mother's face, suddenly splintered
by a song. There's the appointment with the furnace
man, the man with a shovel, the Romanian
raconteur with his hand on her thigh, who of course
has a wife of his own. Between slow dances
to fast songs, there's the woman who asks to see
pictures of the kids (there's more than one way
to refuse skin). There's the woman driving and driving,
one way filling her ears, the other emptying her eyes.
There is her tiny husband, the visiting chef. There's the way
dinner used to be, surrounded by an entire Mariachi band,
and supper now, which starts with no grace and ends
with him backing down the driveway, shaking his calendar
out the window. There's a winter with no kisses in it.
There's a loneliness that fits like an expensive shoe
she didn't mean to buy which may take her somewhere.
There is no other way to say a certain December dawn
but in lipstick color: pink ice. There is the way it finally
allows some baby blue, this cold world for one moment
at her feet.

Hypothermia

I'm driving a cold road, the needle
on empty, the last sign of life miles gone.
Or my foot's mashed in iron teeth meant
for coyote and for once my voice
is too small. Either way, it's the air

that will eat me. Where are all the dogs
and the loyal people who walk them?
No lights or whistles, just a sneaking
certainty windchill is after all not simply
theoretical and no one but me

will people this dream. I wanted to stay
home. I wanted to feed the fire and point
the finger. (True or false: the enemy can only
be death. All of the above, and his sidekick
pain.) I'm thinking of everyone warm,

watching the news—some guy saying:
if caught in a snowdrift, cling to a web
of complexity. Each thread keeps you
awake a little longer: recite the recipe
for lamb couscous without missing a spice,

or the names of everyone in sophomore history.
The sky is reeling, I know it, in the dark.
Who is the enemy? A man in prison for life said
hope. A lawyer said junkfood. Breast implants.
Why does one cat dip her paw to catch the drip

while the others lick from the rim of the drain?
Why is it once you're a mother you say things like

"Where are your socks?" Who invented the term
freezer lamb? The enemy is a bad smell, a microbe,
we'll never isolate it. I am still awake!

Think about the way the center line disappears
around a curve and appears as if unraveling
vertebra by vertebra. Is there such a thing
as a healthy lie? Logic says no one is coming
so I turn it off. I conjure a grocery store log

and burn its gaudy colors in the faux chimney
of my synthetic jacket, all the while
pulling up a wooden bucketful of Portuguese,
the subjunctive of fifty irregular verbs.
The enemy is anyone who brings ugly

intentions anywhere near my kid. Any kid.
Any kid can be the enemy if he's enough
despised. This is when it happens.
If I'm driving, a deer rises up
from the Rorschach of oil or ice on the road.

Who will survive the next collision?
If I'm nodding in the crystalline leaves,
chained to my wound, slow footsteps
approach. A dark figure bringing warmth
or the weapon of his thoughts?

The enemy is man-made.
The quaint term cottage industry
comes to mind. What's that, old body,
light in a window or a dark hand?
If I close my eyes will I freeze or wake?

Quarry

It's about serious digging, near-rhymes
with worry. A job on this scale deserves music,
accompaniment, good insurance—but most
of us begin alone, uncovered, in the dark.
I can't see but I quarry, I presuppose, I mean
to carry. Mine is the quarry of unmarry,
I'm wanting deep water, clear, no more
dead body. Rising out of icy blue, something
almost lovely, unblurry.

Simultaneity

I splash my face, a woman somewhere kindles
her fire. One man is forty stories high, cleaning
his gun, another rakes someone's leaves.
My copper beech releases a dozen more curled
claws, A.'s body hasn't yet made up its mind.
Snow falls on the rug the cat shat on and Della's
getting faster on her crutches. She wants to know
if things smell in my dreams; I'm glad three aromas
are gone from this house. Winter is here with its own
stone, the back steps will stay broken teeth
until spring. I forgot to call Dad about Mom
and Della's out in the dark writing "Kyle" in the snow
on the rug. She tells me the story of G.'s best friend,
dead from a hockey puck; I tell her how L.'s daughter cut
herself last night. The radio says the tigers
are holding an olive branch and the pilots threaten
to walk. Two women I love are exactly the same amount
pregnant. I refuse to think about money, wonder whether
the pumpkins are frozen to the ledge, how the morning moon
hung pale and broad over the chicken house, how
I'll get through next week. They announced a cease-fire
to get polio vaccine to the villages—buying
boy soldiers on both sides two more days of life.
I dry my face and let the cat out of the cellar.

Back Half

A minute after the flash of bounding cat, I know
I've seen longing, its back half so badly wanted—

I'm tempted to say *deserved*—to be fox. Driving
the next curve, suddenly fine gravel distracts me

to hair I didn't know I had on the back of my neck,
and two old skids, bicycle and car, in that order

and a decade between, Shelter Island and Florianópolis,
leg seriously strawberried vs. head-in-lap-on-curb.

No curbs here, just beaten grass or tire-tracked mud
between cars and front doors, many with flags

announcing the next holiday, as if we'd forget.
Voilà: I'm tangled in the word aesthetic, whether

by its nature classist, whether those flags are not,
and then there's a rat belly-up in the margins of traffic,

paws of frozen entreaty, windows of the nearest house
unsympathetic—alarmed—and my heart tending

to agree. A rat in Westhampton, MA—village of pure,
fabulously trained dogs? The way the truth can bound in

or tiptoe past, in a pointy sheet or a loopy rug, smoke
around its shoulders, no name tag, x-rays, dental records.

Poof! The way hope can change jobs, slow to glacial,
forget the right questions. Silly me, to forget

that the dimmer switch is in plain sight. Wise, to learn
the new guy's game is not mine and we wouldn't please

each other with words. How can so many hours
of snowflakes measure only an inch? The truth

would like to be unfettered, just go naked,
but the world is cold. In winter our skin-smells live

in the air pocket under our bundling, the truth
of us emanates only slowly and through cloth.

I can't decide if it's okay for *today* to be rehearsal,
I know once in a while the truth wears bells.

A woman I know called me *creature* twice
very naturally and I ate it up. I wish I could

love her—but my back half has its own
velvet truth, unsatisfied and fox.

Check West Window

I'm not used to waiting out the big storms alone.
By lantern-light, I read a diatribe on the "I" in art.
Check west window, then south. Remember a bolt
zapping my twelve-year-old body into weight-
lessness and half hour later the Armogidas' house

made twice its size by flames. Now the cats are in,
tub filled, no one but me to oooh and ahhh at each
clap, each chrysanthemum of thunder. Let's grant
H. his politics *and* beauty, O. her precipice of self
—let it *all* be poetry—and listen to the drilling

rain. What are ideas if they don't knock you off
your chair? Why not step out into possibly electrified
grass to bring three roses to shelter? Bottom line,
it's not *smartest* I want to be. I want rickety me and
my garden to weather these weathers, remember

those who don't. And, you, reader? Do you think
feeling belongs at the bottom of the food chain?
Without these years of uprootedness would my "I"
have gone underground? Begun speaking in tongues?
No—even when we're not the center of the storm cell,

there is a lashing going on. What are windows for?
When there's major thunder the next town over,
bright forks of light illuminate our back yard,
anything that matters, danger that blasts us scared
and free—without charring our best climbing tree.

What It's Really About

I'd plumbed the clouds, touched down on
seven continents, convinced a ladder

was what I needed in this dream of a dream.
Something wooden with history and sway,

a getting there that could be lowered to a kinder
angle than up, could cross a ravine, casually

lean. Morning said not for climbing, not even
for real—a detail from a painting would do:

blooming from dark brushstrokes a tiny ladder
of light, humming with splinters, tweezers,

eighth notes, faith in tremolo—a highway by inches
like what the eyes do. What the woodpile says:

each going out lives beside an up-in-smoke.
Pool ladder, fish ladder, rope. The underwater

way to treehouse, hayloft, later each other's
bodies. Path of ladderbacks, train tracks,

unbidden memory. The ladder our one-year-old
toddled up when she was ours. There she was,

serene, studying rain gutters. Now we learn
the sign for parallel—a rungless ladder. Your

house, my house take turns holding every noise
she makes, moments she's pinned to one

or another rung. Having to imagine how to go on
and going on—despite the hacked bodies of yews,

the newness of two-ness, the certain deep a certain
boy threatens to fall into—because note by note

it's the air she's climbing. And falling through
the air, a carillon of pollen: yellow light.

FIVE

Throat Ember

Shiny valve by valve the woman shakes
saliva from her French horn. I must have
seen this. I put her in the movie.

In my throat. A ready ember.
She is the red cloth they use
on stage to mean blood
after the body receives the wooden sword.

How can that stalk hold a bird?

The eight-year-old that was me looks to the ocean.
Her toes are dusty with dander of sand,
tough and bare as any part of me
will ever be. Awake, she floats with ease
and touches snakes. Asleep, she is terror
running from a man who has no face,
blank pink skin. I am six times her age
and he looks to me like a big penis
wearing a hat.

Father looked as sure of himself
as ever. None of us knew of the part of him
that was wondering which part of him
would out-shout the rest tomorrow,
and would he fly the plane alone?

A reef is a hurting and a way not to drown.
The brass of the horn is its own gleaming.

The mother I have made for myself
says: apply yourself aslant.
When the nun walks out
of your body, hold her by the shoulders,
say: many are our paths. Mother's face

gives me to understand this.
Tells me I can open as easily as walk.

When I was twice the age of the barefoot girl,
I dreamed every month of standing
on the median, rattled by the whir of traffic.
Always from behind came a knife
for no reason
and a burning that was I knew
the way it would feel.

In the delicious dark of the movies, I have
no body. Sometimes I forget
my elbows for weeks at a time.
The day I felt the knife from behind in *Catch-22*
right there awake in my seat I knew
the dream would not be back.

A man on the radio says: the world
wears irregularity
in an unexpectedly orderly fashion
(lightning, earthquakes). The man
says fractals, says weeds and synapses.
I am asleep. His breath stirs
the hair on my arm.

Dream ember, new shine.
I brush the back of his hand
against my throat.

It's the bird's song that lightens
the stalk's load.
The worst things that have happened
I didn't know to fear.

The Long Moment Before

It's a boat, it's a plane, it's remembering
the male body. It's *I'm not sure I'm there yet,*
caught between wanting and dispensing with.
Before is a place forever in bud. Popcorn
as seed, as scorching, the long moment before.
There are dishwashers and sunsets here as
anywhere, simply no satisfaction, no death.
It's a level playing field rained on by boredom
that teeters over the abyss. Some of us live
uncheered by the lock, others in fear of the key.

New Doors

Monks chanting:
   the way they share a wave-length
On some curve of the earth twelve pairs of feet
   pad the dirt path to the monastery garden

Today is the day for the brother
   on probation
Inside his brown robe,
   inside the droning, a door opens

An interior crevasse blooms
   green with songlight
Door to humility
   and miraculous peas

Some constellation of you and I walk
   through clouds to a sullen farmhouse
The door opens and we're flooded
   with heat and new bread

The door of St. Frances Rest Home is flung open
   to let a man leave, not dead for a change
He breathes risk with his oxygen,
   Aegean blue with his eyes

Door in the small box that is my heart
   resting warm on the mantel
All that new is: sudden chord
   brought by wind or a rash glad hand

Door we give to my father: flight instruction
   (Mother is beyond thresholds)

Door to the sites of myself I don't visit:
   center of gravity, daybreak, torn butterfly

Door to the moon, who doesn't need to be there
   to be there
If you slide to sleep to the right music,
   you wake on the other side of a door

Mind Over Matter

So the next time I chose carefully: masonry.
The good rhythm of scoop and slap. In the morning
my nails were broken but I was well pleased, god-like
almost. By lunch I saw what my sleep had made:

a beautiful wall between me and me. Not the desired
result, but hey I'll find work for a trowel so at home
in my hand. Tomorrow it might be an object
of beauty. One night I approach the blankets

with blueprints under my arms, another I just need
to take off my helmet and lie down. Sleep: courage
or thorazine of the basically balanced—don't we all
have to damp down our inner extremities at times, the way

our manic moments eat up everything in sight and never
without the flip side in hot pursuit. If for me headlong
isn't chemical—just a matter of temperament—
does that mean I have a choice? Can anyone see me

selecting serene for more than an afternoon? Ah, but sleep
I've always been able to own. So I put the little red
colonial we coveted for years with its lilacs and beaver
pond, I put it under my pillow where the couple dressed

in dry-cleaning can't slip it into their briefcase with an illegible
signature before our mouths have closed, and I get a good
six hours, my face pressed to the ancient wood in its heart.
The rest of the week's unfenced hours are filling fast: I'm set

to swing fearless and pre-human in the monkeys' loud
green canopy, I'll immigrate over water wearing sweaty
cotton, play hard with silver filigree, and, by Friday,
fire a hugely ugly gun. Impossibility is all I'll slaughter.

Mykonos, Mattincus, Maceió

It's bone simple to be in three places at once
if some part of you understands bodily
rhyme. Mykonos, Mattinicus, Maceió—
I am behind myself and ahead, at once
moody and clear-skied—everything equals
wraparound sun. What's down the road
looms up slowly, photogenic, in the lens of self:
goats amused by their own beards, gorgeous
rusted hulks hung with buoys, boys shinnying
for coconuts and showing their teeth. I am
the camera. My battery is song. None of these
languages is mine, but I move in them, stumbling
and hungry. Look how I needed these salty waves!

Best Barns

I like them best when they're still really barns,
well-used and smelly as now. Right now
the tips of trees are trying to tell us
that lavender mums lie. I like lying best
when it's out loud, not some kind of pastel
petal impersonator. As if this season
could be suave! No wonder man invented
plastic, nature's such an operator. Looking
out the window, there's a lot of green
to go around but the brights are gaining.
I never really liked orange but I like it best
dirty, no longer pretending cheer. Just as
freshly-painted barns need not apply.
You want to dress up *barn*—add *dance*.
Which I like *best* (hold the fiddles *&* sawdust)
in my realist mode: no partner, no eye contact—
call me selfish but not sentimental. (Glances
like flies on a flank are another story.) I have
this need to shake my body together with you—
and you and you—alone. True may not be happy
but it's multiple best. Like cold wind that likes
warm flesh. Like how aging is learning to go
to your own well. Like that field of horses, all
of them with their heads plugged into the ground.

Dead Rat

Almost skipping downhill
after work, I notice the dead rat
is gone from its spot. I miss it,

and wonder who finally took it
where. I must have walked past
a dozen times before registering

what it was, then another dozen
before nodding, the way we do
once we know someone by sight

if not name. Then we graduated
to the greeting phase: Good morning,
little dead thing, I'm off to the office,

ugh. Or: You're looking more rusty
can today than scuffed leather, dear.
For the rat appeared (I forgot to say)

from the beginning, at least of my
noticing, juice-less, hairless,
less slumped rodent than flattened

armadillo. Why are we drawn
to our friends? Did she make me feel
beautiful? Lucky? Alive? I told her

about the cascade of white flowers
on my road, suddenly ruined one day
by the appearance of a tiny American

flag. The way she continued to lie there
said empathy, outrage. Could anything
be less nationalistic than clematis?

We understood each other. Naked
as she was, not exactly intact,
she had integrity, the quality

of being precisely herself. Her time
underfoot seemed privilege rather
than misfortune: no matter

that she lay downwind of barn—
police horses stabled there—the path
was hers. Oh, where has she gone?

Was it by hand or hoof, accident
or design? Finally I reach
the endless parking lot, climb

into my car, remember her last
words to me: So, are you ever going
to quit smoking? Love a man again?

Separation of Powers

Leave the poor brain alone, it's trying.
Remember it lives in the dark.
This month alone it's learned to surrender
its chair, dared to take catnaps, tried
to hear blood-thrum as music.
Consider the humility in this, so soon
after a demotion. You'd expect at least
a little passive-aggressive fallout, a slow-down
in the department of pros and cons.
Maybe the brain never wanted to be CEO
or referee, actually prefers the role
of consultant and the weeks off on the chaise.
It's a glamorous job—silent partner, unnamed
source—the brain can wear silk and be
indispensable but have a life of its own.
As if divorced and still co-parenting, the brain
and the heart are learning it doesn't work
to each hold one rein, they must wait their turn.
Then one day, eyes wide, without a word
they both let go at once. Something
feels good they don't understand.
Who is she dancing with? Who's leading?
It can't be the feet. Omigod, it's the music!

My Voice

Ever since I began moving
around inside a Bach cantata
air is water and I float.
Dark days, music is antidote;
when it's bright, gloriously
redundant of sun. The sound
from my mouth makes space
instead of filling it: sudden
clearing where a building
has long been. Watch it
take the smoke out of me.
It is an eager, sloppy child.
Begins on a rock as the bark
of a sea lion and becomes
her amazing wet grace.

One of the Ones

I will not forget the body, and that's final.
I will not forget the edge in the voice,
its intentions. I will not forget
the music on the breeze, I will be subverted.
I will not forget what's under the snow,
the bandage, the rug. I won't forget
her forgetting, how one day to fry a pork chop
was beyond her. Or that the matches lie
ready in their flowered tin beside the stove.
I will not forget that we are less
because we decided not to be more.
I won't forget you and you and you, each
with a brutal truth to send away
in a little boat, let me be one of the ones
to keep it afloat, I'll remember.
I will not forget to be defiant, ha.
I'll not forget that remembering is money
well-spent—no: money in the bank—remembering
can be certain and gentle like a mother's hand
in our sleep, a hand that knows we will move
in strange ways when we wake.

You Can Tell

You can tell it's spring—they're moving
    the trees again.
Today's shoes are looser.
In a house nearby a rational man
    reads of dreams.
Plato rides around with him in his car.
Last night we sat watching four men
    labor with bows.
The 1st violinist's left foot kept leaving
    the floor.
Our arms knew our shirts were touching.
Afterward, alone—the mile on foot into pitch,
    the wet wait, the tow truck, the bill—
    all managed to be where I was.
This morning I hurried Della into her shoes
    without an edge.
One more day of balmy and the patches
    of sorry grass in my yard will equal
    the islands of old snow.
Down in the valley they are way ahead,
    with rashes of purple.
Today I will notice every white car.
Music is more and more different.
Why quarrel with slow when it comes
    with laughter?
Moving trees requires faith and keeping
    their feet wet.
Whatever leafs out will be the right kind.

ALICE JAMES BOOKS has been publishing books since 1973. One of the few presses in the country that is run collectively, the cooperative selects manuscripts for publication through competitions. New authors become active members of the press, participating in editorial and production activities. The press, which places an emphasis on publishing women poets, was named for Alice James, sister of William and Henry, whose gift for writing was ignored and whose fine journal did not appear until after her death.

TYPESET AND DESIGNED BY LISA CLARK

PRINTED BY THOMSON-SHORE

Recent Titles from Alice James Books